# Sipping from
# the Writing Well

*Martin van Houwelingen*

Author: Martin van Houwelingen
ISBN-13: 978-1500712334
ISBN-10: 1500712337

*Martin van Houwelingen*

# Thanks to:

Laura - for editing
My friends - for putting up with me
Wendy - my wife and confidant
and
Neil Gaiman - for all his support and encouragement.

# Contents

A word from the author ................................................. 9

1. About writing................................................... 11

2. My history as a writer............................................ 13

3. Writing Well ..................................................... 19

4. The boy, the girl, the story...................................... 26

5. Getting down to it............................................... 36

6. Cutting up your baby............................................. 40

7. Editing .......................................................... 43

8. Cover art......................................................... 49

9. Publishing! ...................................................... 51

10. Getting noticed ................................................ 55

*Martin van Houwelingen*

## A word from the author

Yes.

*Some more words from the author*

Through the years of writing stories I found logic to my style and checking with many famed authors, I found some of them held true to my idiom as well. Quickly I became obsessed not so much with the stories, but with the style and shape of them and for a while there lost the ability to actually write.

In contrast to popular belief, writing is not just about technique. Writing is about having a sense of knowing which word belongs where, what to do and what not to do to make a sentence flow, what follows after something has happened and to get the story told. If you don't have this then please become a journalist, write travel or cookbooks, combine another hobby with putting words on paper and tell people about the discoveries you have made. If you have a sense of storytelling, the urge to have people listening and hanging on your every word, then become a politician.

The longing to create worlds from air, have visitors walk through of them to marvel and be amazed, and the undying sadness when you cannot reach this. When you find the stories popping up in your head, pushing against the sides of your skull, wielding pickaxes and drilling holes trying to get out, that is when you will need technique to make the stories in your mind behave.

If you have this affliction, then for you my friend I wrote this book.

Hopefully you will find my guidelines for writing helpful. They are not rules or commandments set in stone. Please feel free to follow your own heart when you disagree and create your own style. Every god of a universe creates after his and her own image and not from someone else's, though fan-fiction can also be a very worthwhile and fulfilling hobby to pursue.

But a writer who creates something entirely new is unique in his or her own way, with their own set of morals and guides, their own discoveries to be told.

Write, and write well.
Write when you are happy.
Write when you are sad.
Write when there is nothing to be had.
Write when you are longing.
Write when you are full.

And if there is nothing left to write,
then go to bed,
and dream.

# 1. About writing

Knowing a lot of writers, I know the first thing they tend to turn to is look at how to get published to see if they can learn any neat tricks. Though I commend you for your tenacity which made you start with chapter 1, it is chapter 10 you are looking for. But I do wish to warn you that in doing so, you run the risk missing out on useful tips that might help you prevent publishing a low standard book and be disregarded or disappear in the maelstrom of books out there.

Having dealt with that topic, I will start at the beginning.

## *Why we write*

Writing is part of many of us. It is an innate wish to chronicle what is on our minds and leave something behind when we are gone. It's a bit grim, but true.
When I meet another writer, generally the first question asked is not 'how far along are you?', but rather 'how are you doing, you look like shit.' Writing is hard work. A writer who doesn't look like he has spent nights up fretting about his plot, frustrated about word choice and irritated by sheer lack of sleep, is indeed a writer though unlikely an author.
Though the dictionary does not make this distinction, I say that everybody writes but being published makes you an author. It means you have accomplished something, brought the task to completion, an accomplishment worthy of a title, because writing is indeed hard work. Publishers and readers often forget how long it takes to write a decent book, the toil of hours spent writing, rewriting, editing, proofreading and rewriting again. But most writers cannot help it. They are born with the ability to see stories all around them and shape them into a new story that has never been told.
A good website that is selling E-books will have to do everything in their power to aid the writer in completing the quest of writing a novel, because without the novels they have nothing to sell. Right now the writer is in control and can even earn a decent income from their work, if only to buy enough coffee to write the next book.

To divide writers and authors into grades, my second question is most often 'how many hours a week do you spend writing?' The answer to this is in my eyes equal to the chance percentage of a writer to become an author and of an author to become recognized. If you spend ten hours a week on writing, which is one and a bit hours per day, you have a ten percent chance of completing your book, publishing it, and again a ten percent chance of being bought. On the whole this is not a bad percentage. If you write a hundred hours a week, by seer tenacity you are certain to publish and you WILL be noticed, if only by the sheer volume of books you are putting out!

So my advice to you is to write and write every day. As Neil Gaiman, a frontier visionary and well known writer in the genre of fantasy, said: 'Keep writing, and FINISH THINGS'.
Start on a book and stick with it right to the end, even if you think it is complete rubbish you are writing. Remember that you are no longer catering to please the taste of publishers but are writing for the individuals who will pick up that book, read it and like it. Someone out there just might think you are the cat's meow, no matter what you wrote. You can write through preset scripts to please large audiences, but a lot of writers do exactly the same which makes that corner of the market small and too tiny as there will always be people better than you unless you have the inside track and actually know someone in the business willing to put their ass on the line for you.
And so I advise you not to take the easy road and write generally, but write specifically, in your words and your style. You might just be the genius the world has been waiting for, or a fun read for someone with a mind like yours.

## 2. My history as a writer

To explain how I see the world and why I think a certain thing should be done a certain way, you need to understand a bit about me. Those of you who are in a hurry to get to writing can skip this chapter, move on to the next and mark my comments as read. But if you are looking to understand who you are and why you often feel so alone, you might want to keep reading.

### Watching and Discarding

I chose to learn more about how others write, discarded all their ideas and theories of what made a good book and tried to do it my own way. I got a lot of critique from my proofreaders on how hard it was to read, how my lines were too long and overflowing in punctuation, how in discussion it was hard to keep track of who said what, on not to use strange and foreign languages when the main character didn't understand a word that was said.
And I listened and learned. I fought every critique with passion and felt lousy for days when someone had said something mean. But in the end I buried my hatchet, forgave the speakers and apologized for my abuse towards them while they were just trying to help. I even got to the point where I told my proofreaders on forehand that I was likely to yell at them, but to please be honest and kind in their comments.
Through all of this, and it took me years since writing your own way is not something you learn in school, I learned how not to write. After much trial and error, hating people and sleepless nights, I learned how to write. It was still my own way, my words and my stories, but I learned how to use these comments to my benefit.

### Wearing the Writers Coat

To me, writing well it is a lot like having a coat. As a child someone gives you one when you need one. You don't like it, it's stupid and all wrong. But you learn to live with it and learn to like it. My first 'coat' was a library membership card. Finding the library an ideal place, I was never much into sports or very social, I read every book in the children's section. At first I read at random, but after a while I started with the A's and literally worked my way down to the Z's. This got me noticed by a librarian who, when I got stuck in bed with the flue, took the time to bring me the next stack. By the time I was twelve I had read every book I was allowed to read and read my favorites up to five times. Because there simply wasn't anything left to read, I had started writing my own stories which mostly were fan fiction sequels. After a lot of begging I was allowed an upgrade from my junior card to an adult card, with the librarian keeping an eye out so I wouldn't borrow anything that would be... risky. I still own that card, and it has a hand written 'pre' before the word adult, with the librarian's autograph as a sign of approval. When I talk to parents, I can never stress the importance of that library card to them. Not all children take to reading like I did, but there are some out there who, like me, need it to make some sense out of this big weird world.

And so I arrive at the second coat.

The second coat is one you choose. You have grown out of the first one or wore it to shreds as you actually started to like it after a while. But when the world opens up to you with a whole new library to read, this time a hundred times larger as all kinds of genres are at your fingertips, you start to choose and pick.

## The Library

With my pre-adult library card I knew where I wanted to be. While most kids still stuck to the comics, I made a run for the fantasy and science fiction section. I read J.R.R. Tolkien's The Hobbit, Lord of the Rings and Silmarillion, Larry Niven's Ringworld, Frank Herbert's Duin saga (which in my opinion got a bit tedious around book four), Orson Scot Card's Enders game and sequels, Isaac Asimov's I, Robot, Robert A. Heinlein's Starship Troopers (which is a hell of a lot better than the movie, which is good for completely different reasons), Douglas Adams Hitchhikers Guide to the Universe... I read everything. When I got to know their styles and humor, I changed as a person. I learned I could think outside of the box and everyday life, and wrote my first novel at fifteen on my dad's old typewriter. It wasn't a masterpiece; a mix of fantasy and sci-fi in which an Elf-like race was able to time travel but were always rooted to the same place as they tried their best to control the fate of other races by being revered as gods. They found that the more they intervened, the more mixed up the future lines became.

At fifteen I actually did a speech at school about the problems of time travel and causality. For my efforts I was graded a mere five out of a one to ten scale because the teacher just couldn't follow my reasoning in diversifying and shifting timelines into parallel dimensions. Generally teachers didn't like me much as I always had an opinion about everything, but having read a wider spectrum than most of the teachers I was not put in my place as easily as other children my age. I was able to defend my comments on why he adventures of Tom Sawyer was total crap by using examples from other books and explain how in the time the book is referring to, Huck Fin could never have sailed down a river with a black guy for very long. Having watched a lot of American television and comparing Tolkien's Lord of the Rings in Dutch next to the English version, by this time I had taught myself a basic working knowledge of the language and learned more as I studied. English was the only subject I was actually interested in as it broadened my horizon in being able to read more. I got as far as reading Voltaire's 'Emile' when my English teacher noticed my passion and put me through a more rigorous track of learning. When I was asked to read five books for my final year, I just politely smiled and asked if they could be from the same author. Though the teacher frowned, knowing my smiles, he accepted this and I graduated on Tolkien's The Hobbit, the three parts Lord of the Rings and Silmarillion, only slipping and sliding by on the other courses. I didn't write again as there was a strict mandatory book reading protocol in school called 'advanced literature' which bored the hell out of me, but there were pearls to be found, such as the works of Shakespeare. I only found out later that right then I had chosen the coat I wanted to wear and wore it proudly until I was twenty, when I took it off.

At twenty I got distracted by this strange species called 'girls'. I was a late bloomer, but I didn't mind. I was happy and watched movies and TV-series with girls who were as geeky as I was. Being a writer and story teller actually worked in my favor now as I not only knew how to talk, persuade and beguile, I also knew how to sit quietly and listen to a voice coming from a book and think about what was being said, in this case the book being a girl, and make comments, indicating that I indeed had been listening.

## Relationships

Relationships asked a lot from me as I found I was not really suited to be a steady and reliable partner to someone else. I had the skills and could act the role, but in my heart I was a loner with my books as my friends, and when a book was through and the story was over, I continued on reading the next and actually kind of did the same with relationships, always reaching for that star I hadn't touched and shone so brightly and invitingly. As I grew older, I grew quieter and introvert, watching the world from the sidelines as I had always done, but this time aware I wasn't part of that other world in which people laughed together and enjoyed each other's company. Having totally missed the awkward phase of trying to fit in, I had never fallen into the commercialist trap of trying to belong and was quite surprised when other general outcasts made an effort to connect with me. We formed a bond through tabletop role-playing, just one person setting the outline of a story and the rest chiming in with their actions, resulting in either successes or failures at the roll of the dice plus added modifiers for skills which kept the story going.

This is where I actually learned to write creatively, to go with the flow of the characters I was narrating, writing down what they were likely to do according to the situation like Allan a Dale, personifying the writer in his own story, did for Robin Hood and Shakespeare did with Jaques in 'As You Like It'. I never wrote for success, I actually never expect to be read, and hope I will never try. I write because it makes me happy and this is what I still do up to this very day. I do not outline, I do not plot. I just let the story run its course and try to steer the characters in the direction from within the story or from the outside by placing obstacles or solutions, of where I hope to find a conclusion. Sometimes they take a wrong turn and end up being deleted back to the fork in the road, but sometimes they amaze me and create a totally, most often more awesome, ending to the story.

## Weaving

The ability to bend and weave a story is a talent that is highly underestimated as it is considered equal to being able to lie and do it convincingly. To lie with a straight face and the ability to knit different stories together to form a realistic alternate truth can be of great benefit if you know how to properly use it.

At twenty-five I was done with school and started looking for a job, doing whatever I could to make ends meet. I wrote articles for all kinds of magazines on all kind of topics, but never showed anyone as I had grown shy of the world at large. I even wrote them when I wasn't asked for them and just sent them in, hoping someone would read them and publish them. I wrote romance dime-novels for the Doctor Bernhard series, I really didn't care what I wrote as long as I could write. In the end I wound up working at an old fashioned book binder and later at an overnight copy shop which had an Internet connection. There I met a girl from Canada in a chat-room -if by chance you are reading this 'Hi Sue!'- and was infatuated with her spirit, I wove her a romance story which later got the title 'Cloud Castle', the pre-amble for 'Ailin and the Sidhe', the first book I had published under my own name.

## The drawbacks

I have found a lot of writers, like me, suffer from attacks of loneliness and depression. Writing is a stressful thing and knowing the glory and hallelujah of finding the right words, the emotions of feeling with a character coming to life as they sacrifice and overcome, it also holds the pitfall of not feeling anything but emptiness when this glory is absent. We writers are a special breed of people who need others to sit in awe, listen and praise, but at the same time want to be left alone and not be bothered while perfecting our art. But knowing you are not alone in this and that all over the world there are millions of people just like you and me, helps me get by on the darkest of days. Social media such as Facebook help in this regard as it connects us with likeminded people through interest groups, in which from the safety of the keyboard and screen you have the ability to block the bullies and never hear from them again.

## Meltdowns

Every writer has them, and in my opinion any writer who doesn't is not really into the story they are telling. Just like in a romance, after a few months the pink clouds you are floating on start to dissipate, you will see the not-so-silvery linings. It will depress you, you will long to just quit, if only for a while, and take a breath. For me this is usually around page 50, after having written for three days straight in any spare time I could find, ignoring my own needs and everything and everyone around me.

Yes, take a breath, put down the keyboard. Go for a walk, go for a drink, and clear your mind. But the next day, no matter how you now hate the story and still have such a long way to go, sit down again and continue. It will be slow and almost painful, as every keystroke seems to be a lie about what you have felt before, but meltdowns are like that, they happen to everyone. Keep writing, if only for one hour per day. Feed yourself, sleep, do chores, do anything you want as long as you keep going with that one hour a day. Don't falter and go look at pictures on 'IcanhazCheezeburger', as this will not count to fill the time.

Research, write, the next day read back what you wrote and rewrite. Inspiration will hit you in the most unlikely of places, most often when you are absolutely unable to write. Get up from that bed, even if it's the middle of the night and you have an early day, get out of that bath even if the shampoo is still in your hair, and whenever you can, carry a notepad and pen to write things down. A breakthrough should not be ignored unless there is absolutely no way around it.

## 3. Writing Well

'To write is to write well. If you can't write well, then don't write at all'. I have heard this comment so often I almost started to believe in it, but it couldn't be more wrong.

To write is to learn to write, always and forever. You are never done learning and you will always become better than when you wrote last year, last month or even yesterday. You pick up speed in typing, you learn the right way to spell a word, each day you learn. And so I say 'Write, and write often. Even if you have nothing to write about, just write.'

I did adopt the wording 'writing well', as it's referred to in the title. To me it is a well of words, thoughts and images from which everyone can drink. Drink too little and you will be thirsty, words will be hard to type and inspiration only comes slowly if at all. Drink too much and your head will be swimming with ideas and thoughts in which it can be hard to keep your head above water. The trick is to drink just enough and store the extra supply of ideas for later. I keep notepads, one for each story and each one held together with an elastic band, to which now and then I add an idea I have that would work well in this very story. Sometimes different stories wind up actually being the same one and a unique combination is born, a combination only you could create. I generally find that when three stories suddenly combine, the plot becomes visible.

### *Use paper notepads*

Write down the excess of ideas and stick to the thing, or things, you want to focus on. As I am a scatterbrain and easily distracted, I generally work on three stories at a time. While I am writing this particular part of this book in the spur of the moment, in the background I have my current book 'Speechless in Paradise' running on my desktop while in my Inbox I have another chapter of 'Foothold of Tethys' my editor sent me, as well as a story I am editing for a fellow writer who has fallen on hard times. I am always busy, even when I appear to be doing nothing. As I watch movies, my mind is in the directors seat as well as the script writers' and often I comment on where the plot will go, and if it doesn't wonder what the hell they were thinking while making this. And then I spin off into my own thoughts, grab my notepad and write down in a few words the new idea that has formed in my mind. Working on different stories at the same time gives me ideas I wouldn't normally think off and through this each story grows.

## A writer writes

If a writer doesn't write, he or she is not a writer and the writer is only as good as the last thing he or she wrote until after two years what was written becomes part of the collective and is rated equally amongst all other things he or she has written. This means that if you currently have only one book published and want to remain a writer, you need to get your ass in the drivers' seat once more and write a second and then a third one. Every book you write will be better than the last one as you've learned through experience. And so eventually every new book will raise your overall average and deepen the implications your readers read without you ever having thought of putting them in.
 Writing is not always fun. Writing is hard work, sitting long hours in a chair till deep in night, the cramping of your fingers and your mind going so fast that afterwards it will either feel like mush or freeze up completely, in both cases leaving you an emotional wreck.
As Hank Moody summed it up quite nicely in the Californication hit TV series; 'Being a writer is not a job, it is a calling. It's like having the worst boss imaginable. It will jump on you right then and there while the hours you set aside for work are often filled with blank screens and fearful thoughts of getting fired. The hourly rate is immensely low and when you have finished you can only dare to hope that one day you will actually get paid for your efforts. Relationships are hard and strenuous because she will always know you have a passion that rises above and beyond her into something she can never strive to reach. So at the end of the day, when you could do anything else, telemarketing, pharmaceutical sales, ditch digging or being a major league umpire, I would suggest that you do that because writing blows. It is like having homework for the rest of your life.'
I can only say Amen to this, as this is how I regularly feel. But sometimes there is this peek of energy and the words just don't stop flowing from your fingers even though you know it's late and you have to get up early

the next morning. Those are the moments you grab that extra cup of coffee just to keep you awake and keep going as the words feel like gold and everything makes sense. These flakes of gold, these sips from the Writing Well, keep gleaming and raise your spirits when you are down and out, but by chance reread something in editing. Those sips are why I write and why I can never stop writing.

If you have ever felt this, you know what I am talking about right now and if you have never felt this, it is very possible you never will. But that is okay. Not all writers write from passion, some write from research, some write towards a certain audience and some become famed journalists, bloggers or Facebook sensations. It takes all kinds of writers, as there are numerous kinds of readers.

And although it's not fun to think like this, understand that right now, on whatever level of writing you are, you suck compared to who you are going to be. So man up, or woman up, and write, make mistakes, accept corrections or comments from people who you think have the best intentions for you, and grow. It is the only way to become more than you are now.

## Just be true to yourself

Be who you are, not who you or anyone else thinks you should be. If porn is really all you are interested in, then write porn! Who cares! If you believe what you write could damage your personal life, choose a pen-name. But always write from your heart you will always write true and the ones who are like-minded will pick up on it. When you have this, then write what you know, research a lot and make up the rest.

## Take your time

The writing well you are tapping from is not bottomless and frustration can hit you quite unexpectedly. I find a good way to work was defined by John Cleese.

'Take a finite amount of time in which you just sit down and do nothing. Just stare at nothing in particular, and think about what you want to do. Think how you want to do it, think about possible pitfalls you might encounter. Don't be distracted by the things you think up in the meantime, about shopping to do and calls to make. If you want, jot them down on a notepad, but that's it. Empty your mind and think about your goal. And when the time is up, go do it to the best of your ability, again within a certain time frame, and finish. Only afterwards you will know where your weak point lie and through this, you learn to avoid them.'

Sounds simple? I assure you that it is not, but you win nothing by going at it head over heels and trip yourself up somewhere halfway through. On actual writing, Cleese said this: 'In theatre we have a saying 'Always keep them wanting more'. But in this case, you are both the artist and the audience. Set a boundary of time for you to write and stop at the end of it, even when inspiration drives you on. This way you mind can mull over the other things you haven't written yet. You can make notes on good and funny things, but don't sit back down and continue. By keeping inspiration high, you always feel the drive to continue. Sounds silly? Then think of this: When you write until you can write no more, you empty your mind onto paper, which is fine. But the next time you sit down to write, you have nothing to write, the place in your mind you emptied is not filled so easily. This time, you will feel a little frustrated when you start and you will struggle, finishing feeling less than satisfied and drained. Now the time after that and the time after that you will continue to struggle more and more until you have lost the will to write and lack imagining things to write. This is called Writers Block and should be avoided at all costs. Keep yourself interested in what you do and don't eat so many cookies you start to dislike them in the end.'

Brilliant words in theory, but actually having the self-control to do this is another matter entirely. Especially when the world is filled with distractions, some of which, like children, are out of your control entirely, but as a writer, it is up to you to make time to write. Time is always filled with stuff and you need to keep control of that stuff, or be swept away by it. Wishing you had more time and less stuff does nothing.

## Don't mind flaws in your story

If you find a flaw or a problem, see it as an opportunity to create a new way around it. In StarTrek, they found there was no way a big starship like that could ever land and so they invented teleporting. Being at a distance, they needed a way to communicate and so they invented the handheld mobile device while on board the ship they kept talking into the wall mounted speaker!

If you can fix them then fix them, but don't go overboard trying to fix everything. Readers will always be smarter, better read and more inventive in solving problems than you are. If they start to gripe about it, they should try to write their own book. Plot holes exist and no matter how hard you try, you will never pave over all of them. But this doesn't mean you shouldn't try to weed out as much mistakes as you possibly can. Each book has a breaking point after which any editing is just not worthwhile, and that is the time you publish, not sooner, not later.

## Understand your characters

Only if you can relate to what your character is going through, and it doesn't have to be all of it but just the basic emotions, you can write about it. Work related stress is much the same in any job, but it is the job which makes the character interesting. The biggest mistake you could be making is to write about emotions you don't know or understand. A white man doesn't know what it is like to be black, or Asian, nor do writers of those origins know what it is like to be white. When it comes to your characters: when in doubt, don't.

## Research your setting

... but never the main storyline. If you don't really know what you are writing about, sort of like what having sex is like for a virgin, then you can't write it accurately and with passion. Get some experience, get some perspective and then get an opinion, not any other way around. If you can't find a lot or if you are too lazy to do research, then make things up. Follow a decent logical path, or go for completely wild and go all chaotically illogical. But if you wing it, don't refer to it with an existing name. Don't make your vampires sparkle and don't make your werewolves devout vegetarians. Names create expectations and if you cross those, your story will become unbelievable, and not in a good way.

## Don't follow the trends

It seems kind-of logical to write along with a trend when people are buying that stuff and spending money on it. Though by the time you are finished, the trend is most likely over or has already been flooded with similar books. When you notice it for being a trend, it is most likely already on its way out as others have cashed in on it. Take for instance the wizard influx of stories sent to editors after the second Harry Potter book came out was insane! Also stories about zombies, selkies, mermaids, original fairytales retellings, parallel universes, ulterior worlds, time-travel, bad steam-punk, getting revenge, drama just to create drama, pregnancy horror or 'pun and twist' endings are most often found unwanted at the time you are writing them. Be original. Don't just sidestep into a 'what if', but make a run for the border and find what is new and exciting. When you find your creature or race has certain traits which makes it comparative to something already known, then spin it into a different direction. In ' Labyrinth' the character Hoggle at first seams mean for insect spraying fairies, but when they bite it becomes clear that not all is what it seems and he is actually doing a good job.

## Writing for an audience

Though in the first bit I wrote about writing for yourself and never minding the audience, when you get your first book published and start getting feedback and critiques you will indeed start to think differently about that. Accept that the first book you publish will always be a mistake as you are not ready to take on the world, and you will start to write towards an audience.
But to do this you need to understand them and actually be one of them. You need to know what they like and dislike, and with this I do know that a thousand different people can have a thousand different reasons. But when you look at millions of people, you find there are still just a thousand reasons. With word of mouth being just about the best PR there is, you need to remember that people put down books without finishing them because the main character is not likable or even understandable, the writing style is weak and/or littered with mistakes, the story is not within their limits of imagination to understand or even

conceive, the plot is slow or even boring in development, possibly the plot is ridiculous, inappropriate or even immoral. In short, the story is not according to their standards. For each example there are a thousand possibilities, but this is what you are up against and for you to succeed, you need to evade all of the above for a story to reach that chosen audience. No pressure.

But after having read this and having it possibly brought you down, there is one absolute and important thing you must always remember, and that is that...

## You are you

... and you are unique in the way you think and experience things. This means that there is no one who can be a better you than you. Use that. The vast majority of people are not teenage wizards, they don't date vampires, they aren't spies, they're no assassins, they're not involved in political intrigue, and they're not trying to destroy the one ring. Some research can only come from the imagination.
Write what you are passionate about, research what you are curious about to create new possible passions, stay in the flow and when this flow is not there take a break from it all and go out your front door to experience life. Living is the best experience and research you can have.

## 4. The boy, the girl, the story

As I found logic to my style and checked with many famed authors, I found some of them held true to my idiom as well. Quickly I became obsessed with not so much the stories, but rather the style and shape of the story and for a while there lost the ability to actually write. I found many ways to build a storyline but none of them were 'me', as I had forgotten who I really was. In the end I was depressed and downhearted and I tore off pages filled with research, accepting that to write in someone else's style was not the way to go as it had already been done better by the original writer. After a year of utter misery, I picked up the notepad again and wrote a single line: 'The cat sat on the mat.' It was the first line I had ever written in English and I had come full circle, but this time older and wiser.

My point in telling you is this: In contrast to popular belief...

### *Writing is not about perfection*

Writing is a feeling, a sense of knowing what to do and what not to do to make a line flow. His flow is what makes you unique, as only you can decide what to follow with after something has happened and in the end, to get the story told. True writing is passion, love, intimacy and sex, simply by typing or writing down words. True writing brings you to tears while writing.

As I already stated in my 'Word from the author': If you don't have this, then please by all means, become a journalist, write travel or cookbooks, combine your other hobby with putting words on paper and tell people about the discoveries you have made. You work will just be as important as a writer who writes fiction and you will get read.

### *Writing is not about earning*

If you are looking for a quick buck or a cash cow, then please go look somewhere else. Writers hardly ever have any notion of whether the monster they have just created will be loved, hated or disregarded. Writing a book will not make you rich, though it may seem so when you look at the books that are in circulation. Never forget that for each book published there are a thousand books that never made it to the top ten and a million books that were cut short and never published at all. This all also means that your chances are the same as everybody else's, a one in thousands shot for fame and glory.

But if you are like me, then you just long to tell the stories that burn inside of you and derive you of your sleep. Not writing makes you miserable and lonely, an empty shell of a life without your friends on paper.

## *Formula writing*

To write in formula, you have to be aware that, according to Christopher Booker, who wrote a Jungian-influenced book on the analysis of stories and their psychological meaning, there are only seven basic plots to all stories. To write in a genre you need to understand it and have read up on it. Listed below are the seven basic plots Booker has identified in his book.

### Overcoming the Monster

The protagonist sets out to defeat an antagonistic force which threatens the protagonist and/or protagonist's homeland.
Examples: Perseus, Theseus, Beowulf, Dracula, War of the Worlds, The Guns of Navarone, The Magnificent Seven, James Bond.

### Rags to Riches

The poor protagonist acquires things such as power, wealth, and a mate, before losing it all and gaining it back upon growing as a person.
Examples: Cinderella, Aladdin, Jane Eyre, Great Expectations and David Copperfield.

### The Quest

The protagonist and some companions set out to acquire an important object or to get to a location, facing many obstacles and temptations along the way.
Examples: Iliad, The Pilgrim's Progress, King Solomon's Mines, Watership Down, The Wizard of Oz, The Lord of the Rings

**Voyage and Return**
The protagonist goes to a strange land and, after overcoming the threats it poses to him/her, returns with nothing but experience. Examples: Odyssey, Alice in Wonderland, Goldilocks and the Three Bears, Orpheus, The Time Machine, Peter Rabbit, Brideshead Revisited, The Rime of the Ancient Mariner, Gone with the Wind, The Third Man.

**Comedy**
The protagonists are destined to be in love, but something is keeping them from being together, which is resolved by the end of the story. Examples: A Midsummer Night's Dream, Much Ado About Nothing, Twelfth Night, Bridget Jones Diary, Music and Lyrics, Sliding Doors, Four Weddings and a Funeral.

**Tragedy**
The protagonist is a villain who falls from grace and whose death is a happy ending. Examples: Macbeth, The Picture of Dorian Gray, Carmen, Bonnie and Clyde, Jules et Jim, Anna Karenina, Madame Bovary, Julius Caesar.

**Rebirth**
The protagonist is a villain or otherwise unlikable character who redeems him/herself over the course of the story. Examples: Sleeping Beauty, The Frog Prince, Beauty and the Beast, The Snow Queen, A Christmas Carol, The Secret Garden, Peer Gynt, Life Is a Dream

Now these seven branch out into untold millions of options depending on plot, characters and writing style. This basically means that now knowing there are basic stories, you can forget about them and write the story you want to write.

*Streamline writing*

I myself subscribe to streamline writing and don't think about the seven story arches. A story will fit where it is supposed to fit and it is up to the critics and the people who have a need to put things in boxes with a label to figure it out. The following is my own formula on streamlining a story and only time will tell if your way is a good way. If at any point you disagree with my formula, then by all means deviate and create your own. Create your own style of books and become known for it. Every writer is different and so every story, every style and every book should be different.

All I can write about is what I know, so I advise to:

**Pick a Main Character**

... and choose sex, a name, an age and some of the physical characteristics. Though they are not really important, and often I don't even bother to name them in the actual story, they will give you a handhold on who the story is about. All these selections can be changed later when you find it just doesn't work in the story that you created. Should you change any of these aspects, immediately start on a rewrite of what you have written to set the story to its new and improved character.

What is important is that this character must have a reasonable moral compass and therefore is understandable for the readers as they will identify themselves with this person or stop reading. Generally speaking people don't do 'evil' or chaotic things 'just because', they have a reason and it is this reason that makes a character interesting.

**Find the reason**

... why this character is the way he/she/it is. If you can't, you might have overkilled it and need to tone it down or beef it up a bit. If you can understand the character, it is likely your readers will too.

**Create the scene**

Throw the character into a situation you personally dream about, fantasize about, or fear as your reader needs to know right off the bat in what kind of world this character lives. Think of a scene you know something about, possibly your home town or an imaginary world, Google for interesting bits about it for a couple of hours, and then write your first page. Keep the scene and the world it happens in realistic, but let it be interesting, exciting or unusual. This first page is what your readers will read when thinking about buying the book and so it has to captivate. Someone buttering his toast for the first three pages while looking through the newspaper just doesn't do the trick. A need for money or caring for a sibling or child are great, though overly used, scenes as they are believable. Everybody knows that feeling. Find that scene.

## Set the mood

Now think about the mood it is written in. Is this fun to read? A first page about total and utter depression is no fun at all and therefore should be avoided. If writing about depression, one should start on a lighter note and possibly let the character introduce him or herself. Using word-jokes and light comedy, even if it's self-deprecating, always helps to lighten darker moods. Create a problem for the character to overcome.

## Move the scene

Now that the basics are written, imagine how someone with a certain skill-set or mind-set would escape from this problem you created, and block that way out. This will create drama and drama is what you want in your first pages as the character must overcome something and learn something about both the world and themselves for a book to be interesting.
If the created scene is a dire need for money, then why not rob a bank or a post office? Pick the first thing that pops into your head, as it is very likely your reader will a) also think of it and so it will feel believable, even if it's utterly stupid to do, or b) find your idea interesting and new, which is also fine.
What is most important about this are the consequences. When robbing a bank, the police will track them down. The character will run, as a book about being locked in a three by three cell with a guy/girl named Joe/Joanna is hardly interesting. Or is it? What did Joe do to be there? Could he be interesting as well? Will they team up, will Joe hurt your character and with that increase the drama, or will he tell your character something?

Now that you are moving the scene, keep it moving. If it stops, then change the scene by introducing something new and possibly unexpected, good or bad, or let repercussions of something you have written earlier catch up. In chapter five I will go into more detail about keeping track of your story to do this.

**Find the audience**

Think about whom you are writing for and use their vernacular. Don't try to be clever and make up your own words in the hope that you will become famous for thinking of such smart comments as 'flebber' and 'goredamn'... such things are just annoying to your readers. If you are writing for your own amusement, then don't even worry about your audience, as you are it. But when you think the story might be interesting to a certain age-group, choose your words and situations to fit them and how they would deal with certain problems. Where a child would ask a parent for advice, a grownup might not do so out of shame.

**Get outside of the box**

Now when chapter one is done, try to get 'outside' of what you have created. Push your character into the deep end of the pool and bring them to some place they don't really want to be. Doing this will bring a twist to the story. If you somehow have managed to make an interesting first chapter about a man buttering toast while reading the paper, it might be time for work, which is something he dislikes or even hates with a passion. Anything will do actually, but the basic story will be for this person to get back to the place he wants to be, be it buttering toast or going home, wanting to see his mother again which he can't because she is dead... anything will do.
This 'outside the box' is where the story will happen, as magic only happens outside your comfort zone. You don't have to know a lot about this outside world as your character might not either. It is the experience and going through it that counts here.
**Purpose**

The goal of the game is to have your main character survive until the end of the book and through it all having learned something positive.

Keep to regular morality, as they are regular for a very good reason, but don't be afraid to bend or break about five of the Ten Commandments. A story is about adventure, exploration and discovery, not about butter on toast.

## Don't expect yourself to write linear

Sometimes a story has a clear direction, sometimes it doesn't. Accept this. If you know a piece of the puzzle then write it, but keep it where it is supposed to go and make a notation where you left off to continue there when you know more.
The only problem with non-linear writing is that you might know things your character doesn't as you are hopping all over the place. If you hopped, be very mindful of this in the rewrite. Keep checking or even make notes on what the character knows by now.

## Writing is not a Movie

Through popular media such as TV and movies, writers have encountered the problem that they 'see' the scene and the interactions. The problem in this is that you forget to write the things you take for granted, the smell and color of flowers, the feel of the air as someone steps into a room. Write these things into your scenes to create a sense of wonder but take one paragraph to set the scene, don't rant on for pages on end about a field of cornflowers blooming unless that field is the centerpiece of the story. And if so, spread the scenery around. People actually skip pages and lose interest when trying to get to the fun stuff of interaction again.

## Don't aim to confuse

A very well-known Hollywood trick is to confuse the viewer and about halfway through come with some platitude the viewer knows so they can relax and go 'ah, now I understand', while what they understood is the platitude and not the actual story. In books this trick just doesn't work as readers, unlike most people watching a movie, will walk out and put the book down, stating that it is stupid and pointless, or even flip back some pages to understand what the hell has been going on. Try to confuse and you will be found out to be the liar you are.

## Ritualism

Every story has rituals, things that have been done by characters a thousand times before and therefore have become automatic, even ceremonial. Just think about the Japanese tea ceremony. On the whole it is nothing more than drinking tea with someone. But as being alone with someone held certain risks, with it came all kinds of rules and regulations. One shouldn't talk about risky subjects or make improper remarks, and so it was described what you could talk about. Safe things, like the cracks in the cup, indicating they are old and handled with care. It ritualizes how to pour so you won't spill and be ashamed, how to sit, how to drink. Such ceremonies are pure gold when describing a race, whether it is in religion or household chores. You do not need to know why they do so. The race itself could have lost meaning to the ritual ages ago and just do things this way because it works and it has always been this way. If a ritual is logical to readers, it will draw them in and set the scene.

## Just don't

Now that you are writing, there are a few things you should avoid or at least keep an eye on.

1. Avoid writing in first tense, unless you are writing in diary style or doing a personal exposé. Know that it is possible to write in this style, but it is extremely tricky as you have to be funny, witty, recognizable and insightful all at the same time, all the time.

2. Do not write in present tense, unless the events are actually happening right now as they are written. Even then it will be confusing and annoying to the reader, as reading in past tense is much easier. When does someone write chronicles? When the shit has already hit the fan, and not before.

3. Do not switch perspectives. Your lead role is your lead role.

4. Though it is possible for a reader to know the thoughts of this lead role, it is illogical for the reader to know what is on everybody's mind and close to impossible that the main character can act upon this, unless it is emoted and shown.

5. Don't rant. Ranting is going on and on about a particular subject, most often an injustice you feel strongly about. If you want to write about a topic then that is fine, but create a solution and don't just bitch and whine.

6. He said, she said. Be creative in your talking scenes. Work with expressions and body language as you use variations of the same word or synonyms: said, spoke, commented, commanded, proclaimed, pondered, just to give a few examples.

7. Use your dictionary, but only write words you know. Nothing is more confusing than a misused word placed out of context, as it shows that you are trying too hard and seem better than you actually are.

8. Avoid common language mistakes.
Their, there and they're are easily mixed up, but make you look like a real fool when used wrong. Other examples are to/too, add/ad, than/then, your/you're, affect/effect, sue/sew, a lot/allot though never alot, by/buy/bye, sell/sale, lose/loose, chose/choose, bear/bare, brought/bought, here/hear, lose and loose, quite/quiet/quit, weary/wary, weather/whether, wander/wonder, woman/women, principle/principal, soul/sole, complement/compliment, stationary/stationery, due/do, should/would/could, comment/command, hole/whole, the use of apostrophe's such as 've meaning have, and all the 's and ess...

Learn the differences and when to use what. You don't have to be perfect, but at least you should be trying not to stress out your editor.

9. And last but not least, for god's sake and all that is holy, use spell-check! Though it will not filter out every mistake, especially the ones where what you typed is an actual word, it will notify you that something is wrong in about 80% of the cases, which is still a whole lot

better than nothing.

*And be careful of*

... certain words that creep into conversation so easily, but in a book just look awful. Words like a lot, very, really, started, suddenly, amazing, awesome, that, other... These and some other words are words that don't really say anything amazing or awesome, they just hang there, filling up space, and don't really do anything. They are through words, words used for someone who is thinking but doesn't want to stop talking. And writing is not about talking.

## 5. Getting down to it

There are words on paper now, your first chapters are done and the excitement of writing has dissipated. This is perfectly normal. It means that it is time to reread what you have written, edit here and there, possibly everywhere, close possible plot-holes before they spread, open possible new leads to move the story in, add bits you think are just funny or good, and find your way back to excitement.
Now you are actually writing!

### *Start with a Bang!*

Think about what it is like to be a reader. You went to the bookstore or were browsing online, and have found something you like, so you turn to the first page. If after this first page you can't put it down, it is very likely to become a buy. Especially with online sales where the first few pages are open to read for free, this is very important if you ever want to get money out of your writing and use that to continue writing. Though money is not the objective of the game, it can art like a motivation to see people are buying and therefore liking your published work.

### *One by one, introduce the characters*

Let the reader adjust to the order of things and introduce the secondary characters. Don't throw the reader (who is now just you) into a hefty discussion of counterpoints with five people talking at once, as they won't be able to figure out who is who. If you are confused, it is most likely the readers that come after you will also be.
The easiest ways to slowly let the reader sink into the hot-tub that is the story, is through action. A chance meeting or meeting up with a friend, or enemy, or in thought, remembering someone or nervously thinking ahead what to say, what to do and for god's sake not look stupid. But whatever the scene, make sure intentions are clear on how the characters see each other. Arch enemy or combat trainer? Then make it an action sequence while keeping the reader in the dark about who the

hero is fighting until the very end... or not, the reader can discover a lot from interaction and shouts as well, much like the surprise attacks of Kato in The Pink Panther. This is the first real scene after the intro, possibly taking up about four pages, so make it noteworthy. J.K. Rowling did this excellently with Harry Potter and Draco Malfoy in book one, where the two characters met, Draco did his little speech about superiority and right after this Harry openly spoke to whoever was in earshot that he didn't like Draco. Introduction set and at the same time showed the morality of Harry as a fighter for justice and friend to those who are regarded as the lower class: a folk-hero with a legend, against Draco, a highborn brat with a superiority complex.

## *Storyboarding or Pantsing*

Storyboarding is a useful tool to write as you set out the course of the story on forehand.  It can also be a bore as when you are finished, you have already written the basic story and it might not be fun just to put pen to paper as for you it has already happened. So writing on the fly and by the seat of your pants, also known as pantsing, is another way to go. The problem there is that you have no idea where you are going. Learn the differences and when to use what. You don't have to be perfect, but at least you should be trying risk getting stuck in the story or lose interest much easier.

I myself storyboard in my mind as I enjoy it when the characters take me places I had not yet thought of. If you don't set out a path for your hero to follow, it can be a real b...other in the rewrite.

If you feel or fear you are losing control over your story, then it is time to plot out the most noteworthy scenes you envision before writing them. The easiest way to do this, is by writing each scene on a sticky note and place them on a timeline. Now you can shift and shuffle, add en remove them to your heart's content until the story becomes clear. When the pattern is there, some writers use a different color and make those the scenes where things take place. Now you not only have a story line, but also the backdrop. Now add smaller sticky-notes on the scenes for the items and people needed to make it past the problem, post where these items are found on forehand and there you have it, a complete story in its most rudimentary form. All you need to do now is write the things you have seen.

## Mark important information

As I write in Microsoft Word, I use headers to keep track of important information like main character name, his family, important background, intro of other characters and such. They are easy to delete in the editing, but keep my mind on track of what happens where. There are different writing programs out there, Scrivener and the like, but all work on the same principle of setting up markers.

## Confuse and amaze

When the story levels out, add another problem. When you have too many problems to keep track off, solve a few. This way the reader will keep reading, because they want to know what will happen next.

## And keep it real

To me, nothing is more annoying than Rambo pulling a longbow out of his *ss or the quiver that randomly sprouts arrows in of arrows in HungerGames II. Count your bullets, reload when necessary, not just when it is convenient.

## Find the Pearl

During the story, find that paragraph that hints to the storyline and shows setting but not the plot, and mark it so you can find it again. You will need this for your back cover. It should not be on the first page of the story however as possible buyers will very likely read that page as well.

## Grow and learn

A character must learn and grow, or else he would be right where he started in the first place to make the same mistakes again. A reader will find solace in what the characters have learned about themselves, the world around them and probably derive some moral point of view from it. It doesn't matter if this moral is not what you intended it to be as reading is not the same as writing. And after all problems are solved, then...

## End the story

These three words are just about the hardest thing to do when you have lived and loved with the characters, but leaving an open ended story is annoying, even if you solemnly swear to write a sequel. Each book must have an ending and you get to decide what this ending will be and how the reader will feel when closing the book. If you have done well, a reader will long to spread the word on what they have read.

## Use your social media

While writing, it is fun to post little gems of what you have written on your Facebook page or any social media of your choice. It is a good way to share your ability to write and will keep your spirits up when the Likes come, just knowing that you were read. Tell your friends to like the posts and that it helps you to write. This kind of social media actually makes it easier to know if what you are writing is hitting home with people. Where a few years ago writers had no idea if their work was any good and just published, the modern writer can test the waters on topics. The people reading are your friends and if they don't like your writing, they shouldn't bother commenting either. At this stage of creation input is vital to you continuing, but any mean comment can send you off into a downwards spiral, so know who you are sharing with and if necessary, create a different group just for the people you trust. They will like you for it, knowing they are on the inside, the trusted. I personally really don't recommend using a blog for this, as to me a blog is something permanent, a diary kept for prosperity, and not suited for throwing out fishes to make people curious, just like a website is too static and using mail is spam. Facebook has a perfect open chatty style in which everyone can read along what everyone else is doing and eating and disregard the things they don't want to know. Just be careful how much you post. You don't want to bore your future audience or give away too much so they won't buy the book anymore having read it all already, or other writers to walk away with your hard work.

## 6. Cutting up your baby

'I have written this, so now what? How can I publish it?'
I have been asked this question so often I always get a laughing fit when
I hear it again as after writing comes the hardest part: having it
proofread and the following rewrite.
Writing a book is one third of the work, rewriting is a sixth. After this
comes editing and you re-editing the editors work, which takes up just a
little less than the last third, while the last remaining bit is reserved for
publishing and advertising. A good edit takes just about as long as
writing it in the first place as someone else is working hard to correct
your mistakes and polish the little gems you have written into jewels
befitting the crown you will wear.

Because you cannot do this while still enthralled by your own greatness,
I suggest you take a...

### Time out

After the story is written, you are likely to feel drained to the core and
your mind is fixated on the story. Now it is time to take a step back, just
take some time, put the story away, and do something different. Go for
a walk or do the things you have left undone while writing (where
cleaning and the dishes are likely places to start).
Usually it takes about a month for me to get my head back together and
I call this 'the story holiday'. Let the story fade in your mind until the
end of this month and when you feel up to it, start fresh and at page
one. This time the goal is not to write a story though, but to fix it.

### Fix the plot-holes

Much like a newborn baby, it is a little weak scrawny looking potato that
needs constant care to grow and is full of holes the plot is leaking out
off. It might be beautiful in your eyes, but only a true believer will
complement you on a job well done.
After about a week, start at page one and read. Examine it, subjugate it

to close scrutiny. You need to right the wrongs, dot the i's and cross the t's before anyone else can lay eyes on it.

If in the rewrite you feel the story is crappy, then cut it in half at the point where you thought it was pretty good and where it went downhill, and continue from there in a new direction. It will set you back, but it will better the story in the end. And if not, you still have the original. Only when you are thoroughly disgusted by this monster you have created, your story will have grown from a baby into a child and it is time to set it loose in a safe environment.

## Register your work before distributing!

The cheapest way to do this is to mail it through old fashioned postal services to yourself in a closed envelope and have it date-stamped. Don't open the envelope and put it away for safe keeping. Not everyone is to be trusted, and if push comes to shove and someone else suddenly publishes your book, this envelope will give you a better chance of winning the debate in court. Different countries have different ways, but here in the Netherlands I can have an envelope officially sealed at the tax office. The date is registered in an official document and what is inside this envelope is then a time capsule. Once a year, twice if I have great writing spurts, I burn everything I have written onto a CD or DVD and have it sealed, along with my older works, and on the envelope I write what is on there. This way I keep a record of years when something is written in case anything goes wrong, which fortunately has never happened to me.

## Proofreaders Assemble!

Having kept up your social media in keeping people curious, you can now give a shout that you are looking for proofreaders. Just wait for the offers to come in, or give another shout. If nobody responds to your second shout, you are searching in the wrong crowd and need to join a better group of people. Most people who own an e-reader will be happy to proofread and give you feedback as it means they are getting a book for free. It doesn't mean they will read the entire thing, but if you can just get them through the first chapter, they will have a gist of the story and can give a comment or two.

## Proofreaders need to like the genre

You cannot let a hardcore scifi reader read romance, it just doesn't work. Pick your proofreaders carefully and set a date for them to react, even if they are just half way through. Most proofreaders need instructions on how to read though, as 'yeah, I kinda liked it' doesn't really help you. Ask for feedback, tell them to write down what bits (with the page numbers PLEASE) they didn't really care for, what they found confusing and what they loved. Take each comment seriously, but not too seriously.

## Getting feedback is hard

... especially when it is negative in tone. You'll just have to swallow your pride and not alienate the person who was doing you a favor in reading your work. You might need this person for another proofread later on (or not). But no matter how negative the comment was, someone has read your work, which is a start.

## Rewrite

Just start at the first page and read. When you come to a bit a proofreader disliked, then try to see the piece through their eyes. What is missing? Is it too descriptive? Is there not enough description? Is your writing style flawed and if so, in what way? Having coffee with this person is a good idea, but only if you can keep your emotions in check when asking them why they made this or that comment. Your first book will hopefully not be your only book. To be honest, my first books were complete disasters. But through each story I wrote I got a little better at writing. With each comment, no matter how hard it was to swallow at the time, I sharpened my toolkit and increased my knowledge on how to write.

Just rewrite bits *you* now don't like. If you really like something your proofreaders disliked, then never mind them. They have their point of view, just as you have yours. They have done their job and now it is up to you to go through round two.

## 7. Editing

Writing doesn't pay the bills, it just adds to the cost of living and editors are expensive. Every writer struggles with this same problem for each book they have written and there is no easy solution. As everyone is trying to get their bills paid and preferably have something left for luxuries, no one is willing to put down a hefty sum for services not yet rendered. But as you progress in your writing, you will find that the more readers you attract who are actually buying your books, the more expensive good editors will become.
A decent editor is fine to start with, but to actually have a good editor is better in so many ways. Not to mention an editor who has finished a doctorate in English and is perfect in using punctuation. Or is it?

### *Is an expensive editor really better than a cheaper one?*

It serves you well to compare your work in terms of levels of excellence to others and ask yourself: Does a mid-level book really need top notch editing? Would a romance novel be just as well served with a mediocre editor instead of a universal scholar? It is very likely that expert punctuation will kill the flow of a book, as commas and binding sentences together can say more than the words in them alone.
So I'd say no. I don't think an expensive editor is better, not always. Not when editors can make up their own prices and often flog themselves to be better than they really are. This is why writers need to test editors on forehand and take some time to consider and negotiate what is fair as payment for both parties.

### *Always make the editor write in a different colour.*

This way you can keep track of changes and skip through bits that apparently have made it through their scrutiny. MS Word allows you to enable the option "restrict editing", with which you can set restrictions for formatting and editing the document.
You have entrusted your child to someone, but over time this person can grow tired. Even editors with the best intentions can sometimes

drag their feet and not do the best they can do, and it is up to you to catch their mistakes and keep them on their toes. This is true for all editors, not just the freelancers. Give them an hourly rate and they will drag their feet, work slow and bill you for more hours than they have actually worked. To keep them going you will need to...

## Motivate your editor

When negotiating an editing price, always keep a percentage on standby to raise the stakes and keep things interesting for the editor. You may want to tell them regularly they are doing a great job and keep track of their personal lives. When an editor is down or depressed, it is only natural their work will suffer as a result, whether they want it to or not. Never forget that...

## An editor is a person

You are about to engage in a bond of trust and not just work with someone who is there to do something for you. Take interest in their lives, or at least fake it by writing down or copy pasting bits they talk about, so you can ask them how it went later. You delivered them your baby and if you trust your midwife to nurse it through its weakest days. Together you will hopefully bring it to maturity. A writer needs an editor just as an editor needs a writer. There is no other way to do this, so...

## Pick someone you like

The editor doesn't need to really like your genre. Sometimes it is even better for a non-fan of the genre to do the work as the storyline will not distract them. But it has to be someone you can talk with and not just to. I cannot stress the importance of this enough.

## Don't expect miracles

I generally come to an agreement with my editor to do a chapter of twelve to fourteen pages in one week. This means two pages a day on average, which generally takes about half an hour. Know that a nonprofessional editor will only have an hour a day to edit your work, for they have a life as well. Editing for you is not their pride and joy, most of them are just earning a bit on the side while juggling a day-job and a relationship. Expect them to require the same amount of time you have spent writing the damn thing. If you find an editor who works faster and still gives good results, keep them close. These people are precious, so pay them in gold, myrrh and incense if you have to.

## Finish the work together

When an editor commits, they do so for the entire journey as it doesn't work when an editor cuts out half way through. You might as well then return to the original document and go look for a new editor, as work half done, even when it is redone with the best of intentions, leaves gaps and holes in the way the book is read. Smart readers will pick up on that and in the end the editor isn't discredited for it, but the writer is.

## So how much does an editor cost?

Now there is the real question. To be honest, there is no 'going rate'. Any and all editors will try to get top dollar for their work, while you are trying to give them as little as possible and still keep them motivated enough to actually do their job and do it well.

But to answer the question on a personal note: I have paid editors two-hundred euro's for a book of two hundred pages, just as I have paid some a thousand for the same amount of work. All that matters is expertise; how good is the editor and how good do you need them to be to get published. Dime novel readers are quick to overlook a spelling mistake as the book was cheap to begin with and so is the storyline. But when having written an epos or a work equal to Dickens, it would be close to a disaster if the editor keeps mistaking 'there' for 'their'.

When it comes down to money, have a number in mind you can spare and offer to pay half that amount as an opening bid. If the editor blatantly refuses, it is very likely this editor was never in your price-range to begin with. If the editor starts negotiating, then you have a basis to work from. If the editor agrees and the work is good, or good and quick (never accept bad and quick or bad and slow), then offer a bonus. This way everyone is happy. You might have to save dimes for it while writing, but it's worth it.

Now to get to the nitty-gritty, I personally keep my eye on the following list as a general indication of what I consider fair to pay an editor (and yes, I do check references). And by the way, with the Euro, Dollar en Pound so close to each other, fee can be considered in any currency.

| Books edited / Fee per hour | |
| --- | --- |
| 1 | 2,00 |
| 2 | 2,40 |
| 3 | 2,80 |
| 4 | 3,20 |
| 5 | 3,60 |
| 6 | 4,00 |
| 7 | 4,40 |
| 8 | 4,80 |
| 9 | 5,20 |
| 10 | 5,60 |
| 11 | 6,00 |
| 12 | 6,40 |
| 13 | 6,80 |
| 14 | 7,20 |
| 15 | 7,60 |
| 16 | 8,00 |
| 17 | 8,40 |
| 18 | 8,80 |
| 19 | 9,20 |
| 20 | 9,60 |

## *When do I pay my editor?*

Also a fun question to consider. I have seen many different types of payment schemes along the way and when it comes to money, I am distrustful of using "a starting point, halfway there and finish" point of view.

For one, there is the 'we'll get to that later.' I don't think I have to explain that this is just asking for trouble. When you're half way, this type of editor will start asking high rate prices to continue working for you, for whatever reason they dream up, realistic or not.

Secondly there is the 'I am worth every penny' or 'if you don't, you will regret not hiring me' type. As the merging of writer- and editor style is dependent on whether or not the two match, there is no sure-fire way to tell if someone is worth anything without putting it to the test and someone claiming to be worth something on forehand is just blowing smoke. Have the editor proof-edit some pages or a chapter, just to see what they make of your work, and then get into negotiating a price.

Then there is the 'my fee depends on the work that has to be done'. Though this sounds thoughtful and deep, what the editor is actually saying is that if you are bad, they will charge more. An editor is an add-on to weed out (little) mistakes, not someone to do a total revision. Someone completely rewriting your work is nothing more than a writer abusing someone else's work. Though your style will never be perfect, accept it and adapt it as your own. Only a teacher can say what is good and what is not.

'You can pay me per chapter'. Also a fun one, as it gives incentive for spread payment, but the editor can quit or raise prices anywhere along the line, and you will end up with half a document done, which is just as bad as not edited as all, and money out of your pocket for nothing as an end result.

So what is left?

Personally, I only pay my editors at the end of the book, though pay them handsomely for their work, even more then the agreed upon rate. Only getting paid afterwards is not motivating for the editor, so if the editor just works for the cash it is very likely they will do the job poorly due to lack of concentration and incentive. Only a professional minded editor, and I have seen them at a start-up level, will be able to look at the reward waiting at the end of the road and keep pushing to keep you happy. After all, you are just as free to tell them you are firing them anywhere along the line, but do know that people talk. If you cheat one out of payment because you fire him just before the finish line, people will know about it. So be careful.

*I have written, so I can edit (and earn a bit on the side).*

No. To write is a creative process of story lining, creating plot and going with the story to tell it to the reader. To edit is tedious checking of spelling and sentence construction. The two require completely different sections of the brain and often one is developed while the other is not. Very few people are actually gifted on both sides of their brain and those who claim to be have I always approached with caution. Being creative in words is often seen as something anyone can do, but to really write well is a gift you need to be born with. If you write from skill alone, it is unlikely you will display more creativity than a researcher publishing a paper on the work of others.

*Never do your own editing*

... unless you want to look like a complete fool. You cannot see what you did wrong, which is why you did it wrong in the first place and spellchecking will only get you so far. Having someone go over your work with a red marker to point out your mistakes is how you learn and get better.

## 8. Cover art

Now there is a lot of discussion going on about this, whether pictures from the Internet are viable to use, which ones are and which are not. I for one take cover art apart into mockups, a pre-release cover, and the real thing to be published.

When I do a mockup, I use pictures from the Internet. But as no one of importance is going to actually see this temporary cover, I can mix and match to create the look I like. When a book goes in for publishing, I give that mockup to a photographer or artist to get my message across on what I'm looking for and let them run with it. You cannot expect the photographer to read your mind on what you want or read the book to be able to make the picture, so find or create something similar and have him/her make an original.

The real book cover only comes in play when you are dealing with a publishing house, but in all cases the pictures made b others are never exactly the same to what you had in mind. Try to let go of what you had, as it is now unviable, and see what you have received in return. Does it measure up? Is it any good? Does the story possibly need a few bits rewritten to fit the cover?

The point is that...

### The cover is the first thing someone notices

Whether is it is on a bookshelf, in a shop, or on the Internet, the cover makes people sit up and pay attention. The mind can only take in so many words before it all becomes a blur, but a picture can create a question mark in the potential reader's mind.

### The title

... will then create the second question mark as it will hint to the story. A Tale of Two Cities might be intriguing as a title, but if the entire story takes place in the countryside it just won't work and the reader is likely, even if they like the story itself, to feel disappointed that it wasn't as advertised. The cover font and the clarity of the letters contrasting with the background are also important and the title shouldn't be one in a dozen. If you look for your title on Amazon and you find more than ten hits for books with similar titles, then change it. The entire front cover must entice the onlooker enough to read...

## The summery

I have covered this because it is often found on the back of the book, though in E-books the summery is more often posted next to the cover at the site where the book is being sold. It is there to draw the reader in and give them a hint of the plotline, while describing the story setting. Is it sci-fi, a romance novel, or a first person account of atrocities in the Middle East? The reader needs to know to be willing to open the book and expose themselves to more.


It is actually the combination of the cover, the title, the summary and the first page of the book which make the reader decide if they want to buy the book and read on, so they are all equally important. But next to all these, only exposure will get books sold.

## 9. Publishing!

If you have skipped through the book or used the Contents list to get here, I suggest you turn back and read the chapters heading up to this one. It is almost certain you are not ready to publish yet. Really. Continue at your own risk.

So, finally you are ready. The book is about as good as it is ever going to be and every rewrite you might do now will just alter and not strengthen the story. Now it is time to set the story into a final format depending on the publisher's needs, send it in and hope for the best.

To be honest, getting published in this day and age isn't that hard anymore. With the speed of light at your fingertips through Internet, the entire publishing world is rapidly changing and there is no telling how it will turn out. But that is a good thing for a writer who is writing right now. You will be on the front line, able to see the changes happening if you keep your eyes open and an ear to the ground. Right now all I can do is advise you on how I think the publishing world is going to be, from the signs I see.

### *Publishers vs. Self-publishing*

So now we come to this nasty topic.
You can send in your work to an official publishing house, just hope and pray they will see dollar signs and accept it, or you can take your chances on the free market amongst the millions of other self-published books out there with the possibility your story will be swept away by the current and is never seen again.

Often publishers employ their own cover artists and editors, so the cover might not turn out the way you had expected and you might have to pay more just to have it redone. A publisher who does not take quality into consideration is not really worth your time, unless it's in your financial or reputational interest. But then again, most self-publishing websites have conditions on how to deliver your content and cover. Either way you have to be careful you don't finish all your hard work by dropping it in a pigsty, so in the end the choice is yours.

Of course there are exceptions to the rule. You might find the perfect publisher that fits your needs, doesn't charge (too) much and takes a lot of work off your hands, or is willing to accept what you have done as it is. You just might find that retired English (or your language of preference) teacher with nothing to do, who just loves to teach and work with the language so much (s)he is willing to pay you for editing. But in my experience, these are close to insane possibilities and we can dream, but not build a general rule out of them. Yes, both are out there, I have seen them, but they are so rare that they are guarded with intense ferocity by those who found them first.

## Publishers

The general rule of publishers is that it's a group of people working to create books and earn a living from that. As publishing houses have sprung up like toadstools over the years and most often are unwilling to take a risk and invest in a writer, it is actually hard to find a good one. Most of the time you, the writer, end up paying for all the 'services' they offer, which are most often mandatory in a 'take it or leave it' sense. But there is something to be said for them knowing the way and having built the connections to get your book out there. They have eager and accomplished editors, a printing press on standby, cover artists at the ready and advertising houses just waiting for their call. But all of these people and their equipment will eat bits from your pie, your profit, since they want to eat as well. You will pay a steep price to be able to use those connections in either royalties per book sold, in which case you end up with fifty cents per book while it cost well over thirty-five, or get about a quarter to half of the profits, in which case you have paid for everything on forehand.

## Self-Publishing

Because of Internet it is now easy to self-publish, but it will be just you and whomever you are able to draw into your madcap adventure of getting the book out. You will need to find a decent print-on-demand and register an ISBN, an international book number as through this you will expand your sales range through web shops such as Amazon. The publishing houses scoff at this self-publishing, because it is keeping money from their pockets and the reader frets as they cannot find something decent to read anymore that ensures quality for their cash. Never in my life have I seen anyone go online or into a bookshop to buy an unknown book from an unknown writer, simply because they like the genre and are curious. Each book costs the buyer money, money they could have spent buying food, a drink or something else they like.

## E-books

And so we come to e-books. Official publishers have tried to hijack the e-book prices by keeping them just a bit below the price of a pocket or hardcover, but they were just looking for a big payout, while in the writer's contract it still stated that they got paid 'per copy sold'. Though an e-book does need editing, there are no further publishing costs and sometimes not even any cover art involved as most e-book readers still use monochrome or simple black and white.

But this too is changing. More and more e-books pop up for mere pennies and people knowing where to find them are willing to take a risk and download it for low cost. Also through illegal download websites, already bought copies spread like wildfire with no one actually getting paid.

## In the end

... it is your choice which road to take. Publishers don't like self-publishers and even refuse writers who have self-published simply because they can.

First books are hard and just as when you started writing, when you start publishing your first books it will most likely go unnoticed. If you keep at it though, around your fifth book your name might begin to be remembered and suddenly people will be interested in your earlier work.

Keep your hopes and spirits up and write, as that is what you wanted to do in the first place. It may take some time, but when you do what you love, being published is just the cherry on top, possibly with sprinkles.

## My thoughts

In the end the stoic publishers will lose this fight and will either go under or have to change their tactics. Already some have caught on that this mass abundance of books is a good thing, if only it can be regulated the right way. Collecting writers and their books, they are creating a mass market of digital books and offering them at a very low price. Readers can download a mass amount of books, read them or discard them, and comment on the books themselves, creating a database of information. From this database other readers can decide if they think the book is worth downloading.

This is where I think the book market will end up.
If many people find the story interesting, they will buy it and the amount of books sold will indicate a rate of quality while the comments show a person to person view. A book from an unknown writer can be an unexpected hit and the writers get all the earnings directly into their bank accounts. Writers might even be able to register the book with different outlets and get to decide which earns them the biggest profit. Eventually these websites will demand exclusive rights to the work, but will have to prove they are actually able to offer the best chance of success.

## 10. Getting noticed

Getting noticed is possibly even more difficult than writing a novel, especially when it's your first time. But every time you do so, you reach out a little further while giving those who have noticed you before a gentle reminder that you are still out there.  NEVER spam your fan-base as it just makes you appear desperate, or go into personal details about your life as it makes you look unprofessional. Have an off-day? Then don't advertise. But try to do something each week, even if it's only updating your social media pages.

### Social media

Your social media should entice the people around you to read the book that is out there for them to read. Most likely your family and friends will be the first to buy a copy, if not for any other reason than to give you a sense of accomplishment and some money in your pocket. And this is fine of course.
Some of these friends will also share the fact that you have written a book and show that they are proud of you by sharing it on their Facebook pages, but this is just general messaging which you shouldn't expect anything big to come from.
Post little friendly or helpful comments on pages of others, send them a funny music video on their birthday. Social media is all about being liked.

### Chats and groups

Don't underestimate the power chat sites and interest groups can have. If you can find the right one which is regularly full of or has at least a thousand members, you can join and chat along. Be friendly, be informative and helpful, befriend people and get known, get noticed. Not only will you learn from people wiser than you about the subject, it is also a great place to once a week drop a comment that you have published your book. Let those interested befriend you on Facebook, as with more than three-hundred friends interested in you, your friends will grow exponentially through their friends.

## Short stories

By writing some 12 to 20 pages short stories, possibly set in the same world as your novel or the back-story of some side characters in this novel, and giving them away for free as E-books or on your social media, you can create a fan-base that would be interested in buying your novel. Since the marketing ploy of 'befriend, then sell' is quite a new one, it doesn't have to oppose the 'quality speaks for itself' or even mass-advertising for brand recognition.

## Advertising

Though any advertising agency will sell you the moon if you let them, I have actually never bought a book because I saw it on a poster, a leaflet or on TV. In all honesty I don't care for advertising, as I believe a good product should sell itself. But through the war of Getting Noticed, good products seem to disappear in the chaos of everyone shouting that their product is the best, which in fact is all advertising does.

As Neil Gaiman said on many occasions, you get hooked on a certain book or a certain writer simply because it is offered to you by a friend in word of mouth or actual copy, or borrow from a library. Not many people actually go into a bookstore anymore to browse, and those two do often don't buy anything. People who buy go into the bookstore with a set goal in mind, to buy a book they love, or want to collect all books from a certain writer or on a certain topic. This means that to get sold, you have to find people who are willing to spread the word.

## Word of mouth

Most of the books I have on my bookshelves are actually tomes of my past, books I read in the library and loved so much that I bought them to own for myself, gifts from friends, or about a topic I just wanted to know more about.

Especially with E-books, people share what they really like with one another and the selling of books is mostly done to support the writer. And to me this is how it should be. No one should benefit from a product they did not produce, assemble or distribute. And so, word of mouth is still the most powerful advertising of all.

Fifty Shades of Grey was nothing more than a joined blurb of several housewives until one of them took it all, rewrote it into a decent and coherent format and sold it. It was written by women for women, romantic and a little naughty, just enough to entice. I have never seen any advertisements, but over a million copies of the book went over the counter anyway. There was an interest and a market no one knew about and though marketing quickly tried to hone in on this, no apparent equal or better book on this topic or for the same audience sold as many copies.

James Redfield went door to door with his 'Celestine Prophecy' and was ignored for years until the wife of a publisher bought a copy, read it and told her husband that it was marketable. And so it was put on the market. A drove of people interested in spirituality bought a copy and read it, started discussion groups and practiced the teachings in search of enlightenment, so much that after a while second hand bookstores were unwilling to take in 'yet another copy of that damn book'.


For me, the best way to get noticed is to do all you can, each day and every day. Autograph copies for your friends and tell them to talk about it with others, preferably loudly in public spaces. Leave free copies all over the place for people to find, throw low resolution PDF copies around on share sites like it is candy. Do whatever you can think of, but never forget that writing should remain the real passion, not getting published. If you write for fame then you need to rethink your values on writing. There are many easier ways to get fame and most will get you richer than writing books.

But if you are like me and you have the need to write, then write. Write! Damn you, WRITE! ☺

About the writer

Martin van Houwelingen is a high functioning PDD-NOS Autist, born in 1970 in Halfweg (NH), the Netherlands, lives in Amsterdam with his wife Wendy and two cats, and spends his life following the his passions of writing, photography and drawing while trying his best to keep the house in some kind of decent order.

Martin has written stories for books and magazines under various pseudonyms to stay in anonymity, solemnly believing that an artist should never enter the spotlight as mixing art with money only results in lesser quality to get paid. The problem in this is that when not being named, fans will search high and low for more but will never find it in the multitude of text that is out there. And so with a heavy heart he stepped into the limelight to show people who he really is and leave his mark for the future generation of writers while sticking to his morals.

These days he runs several Facebook groups to help others to write well, be noticed and get published.
https://www.facebook.com/groups/authorauthor/
https://www.facebook.com/groups/60secondsofcritique/

'Following a life of passions is not something everyone is cut out to do.
It means sleepless nights, constant distractions and mood swings, all while trying to make rent and have enough left to eat.
But if you are like me, with stories bursting in your mind and you only can be truly happy when you are creating something
that wasn't there before, then I say Go.
Go, do, and come back when you have finished.
Follow that dream, where ever it may lead.'

Other (but not all) works from this writer:

The Witch and the Willows – Dragon Magazine
Cloud Castle – Knightmare publishing pack
Mummy, I want a dragon for Christmas – Dragon Magazine
The Knights nightmare – Knightmare publishing pack 3
The Wonders of Wildlife – Sommersby and Hocks
A life in Freefall – Fantasy Magazine
Limelight – Lovers Heart Publishing
Ailin and the Sidhe – Ardor House publishing
So far away from Home – Independent Publishing
Wanda and the Wanderer, 12 promotional short stories
If I would ever miss you – Lovers Heart Publishing
Foothold of Tethys – Amazon publishing
An Autist view of Scotland – Amazon publishing

Sipping from the Writing Well – Amazon publishing

And there is plenty yet to come